The Magic School Bus®

A SCIENCE FACT FINDER

WHALES

SCHOLASTIC INC.

New York   Toronto   London   Auckland   Sydney
Mexico City   New Delhi   Hong Kong   Buenos Aires

Written by Sue Rosenthal.

Cover illustration by Mick McGinty.
Interior illustrations by Carisa Swenson, Carolyn Bracken, and Ted Enik.

Based on *The Magic School Bus* books
written by Joanna Cole and illustrated by Bruce Degen.

This book is a nonfiction companion
to *The Magic School Bus: The Wild Whale Watch.*

The author would like to thank Hans Walters
of the New York Aquarium for his expert advice in
reviewing this manuscript.

ISBN 0-439-38174-6

12 11 10 9 8 7 6 5 4 3 2   3/0 4/0 5/0 6/0 7/0

Cover designed by Carisa Swenson.
Interior designed by Madalina Stefan.

Printed in the U.S.A.   40
First printing, March 2003

Visit Scholastic.com for information about our books and authors online!

Contents

A Note from Ms. Frizzle

Dear Readers,

Before my class boards the Magic School Bus, I always do my research. I find out as much as I can about where we are going and what we will learn there. With a little investigation, I always uncover a beautiful batch of facts.

When we went on The Wild Whale Watch, I came ready with everything there is to know about whales. It was a whale of a field trip, and when it was time for exploration, my class jumped right in and got their feet wet.

We are excited to share all we have learned from our whale unit. You can use the facts you find here in a report of your own.

Have a whale of a good time,
Ms. Frizzle

The Magic School Bus®
A science FACT FINDER

WHALES

Get ready to dive right into a whale of a tale!

Chapter 1:

What Is a Whale?

What animal breathes air but lives in water; has a belly button but no arms or legs; and can be larger than a dinosaur or smaller than a human? If you guessed a whale, that would be a whale of a good answer.

Whales are pretty impressive. The blue whale is the largest animal to ever live on Earth. The orca, or killer whale, is one of the most efficient and intelligent predators on this planet. And the humpback sings a haunting underwater song that is as beautiful as it is loud. Whales, dolphins, and porpoises all belong to a group of animals called *cetaceans.*

The name *cetacean* comes from *ketos,* the Greek word for whale, which means "sea monster."

Are Whales Fish?

Since whales swim in the ocean, some people think they are fish. But they are not. Whales are mammals, just like dogs, cats, hippos, bats, and you.

Like all mammals, cetaceans have lungs and breathe air. Fish breathe with gills and get oxygen through the water. Cetaceans swim by moving their tails up and down, but fish swim by moving their tails from side to side. Most fish lay eggs, but cetaceans give birth to live babies and nurse them. Fish are *cold-blooded*—their body temperature changes according to the temperature of the water they swim in. But all mammals, including whales, are *warm-blooded*—their body temperature stays about the same no matter where they are.

Get Fresh

All animals need freshwater to survive. But the ocean is salt water. So how do whales get freshwater out of salt water? Mostly they extract it from the food they eat. But they also have very efficient kidneys that help them remove salt from the water they do swallow.

How Do Whales Live in the Ocean?

Some whales live in water that is warm and pleasant. Others swim in colder areas, where the temperature can be below freezing. All whales have blubber, a thick layer of fat and other tissues, which keeps them well insulated.

Blubber Basics

How much blubber a whale has depends on where it lives. The bowhead whale, which spends its life in the ice-cold waters of the Arctic, has a layer of blubber that is up to 2 feet (61 cm) thick. But dolphins that live in the tropics have blubber that is only one-quarter inch (.6 cm) thick.

Whales can dive underwater for a long time, but they must come to the surface to breathe. To be able to stay underwater for long periods, whales store extra oxygen in their muscles and blood. They can also slow their breathing down so that they use less oxygen in a dive.

Champion Diver

The sperm whale wins the gold medal for deep diving. It dives almost 2 miles (2,805 m) down to catch squid. That's as deep as six Empire State Buildings stacked on top of each other! A sperm whale can stay underwater for as long as two hours. Most humans can only stay underwater for a few *minutes!*

How Big Is a Whale?

When you think of a whale, you probably think of an animal as big as a school bus. Many whales are this size—or even bigger. The blue whale can grow up to 100 feet (30.5 m) long! But not all whales are gigantic. The dwarf sperm whale is only 8 to 9 feet long (2.4 to 2.7 m), and at only 4 feet (122 cm) the harbor porpoise is smaller than some humans.

Whales are the largest mammals. The average size of a land-based mammal is a bit smaller than a cat.

The blue whale is bigger than a dinosaur!

Where Did Whales Come From?

Scientists believe whales evolved from wolf-sized animals that walked on four legs on land. These animals hunted on land more than 50 million years ago, shortly after the dinosaurs became extinct. Over several million years, whales' ancestors moved from the land into the ocean, probably to hunt. As the creatures evolved, their back legs disappeared and they developed tails; their front legs turned into flippers; and their noses moved to the top of their heads. If you look at the bones in a whale's flipper, you can still see a shape that looks surprisingly like an animal's paw.

Believe it or not, hippos and whales are closely related. Whales are also related to pigs, llamas, and giraffes.

What Makes a Whale a Whale?

Although whales come in many different shapes and sizes, they all have some things in common. All whales have torpedo- or submarine-shaped bodies with smooth, almost rubbery skin. They all have two flippers that they use to maneuver, and a broad, flat tail called a *fluke*. Most also have a fin on their backs called a *dorsal fin*. And instead of nostrils, whales have one or two blowholes on the top of their head.

When a whale is above water, its blowhole opens and it blows out stale air and then sucks in deep breaths of fresh air. But as soon as it dives below water, its blowhole closes tight, so that no water can get in.

Some whales blow out their stale air at a speed of about 300 miles (480 km) an hour. I wish I could hit a baseball that fast!

When whales come to the surface to breathe, they expel air. The mist that a whale blows out is called its *spout*. Each whale has its own distinctive-looking spout. This cloud of mist helped whalers spot whales and led to the famous phrase "Thar she blows!"

Naptime

How can whales sleep in the ocean and not drown? Whales sleep near the surface of the ocean so they can still breathe. Whales and dolphins either rest quietly in the water or swim slowly while they sleep.

Unlike human beings, dolphins only shut down half of their brains and one of their eyes when sleeping. The other half of the brain stays awake at a low level of alertness and the second eye stays open, keeping watch for predators and obstacles. The "awake" half of the brain signals when to rise to the surface for a breath of air. After a few hours, the animal will reverse this process, resting the active side of the brain.

How Many Kinds of Whales Are There?

More than 79 different kinds of whales live in all of the world's oceans and even a few rivers. The whales are divided into two major groups: toothed whales and baleen whales. Toothed whales have teeth, and include all dolphins and porpoises, as well as sperm,

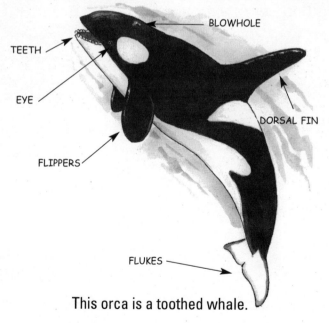

This orca is a toothed whale.

9

beluga, and beaked whales. Baleen whales include the big whales like the blue, fin, and humpback whales, as well as a few smaller whales.

Baleen whales get their name from *baleen*, a material they have in their mouths that helps them strain food out of the seawater.

Toothed whales and baleen whales are believed to have descended from a common ancestor. They split into two different groups about 30 million years ago.

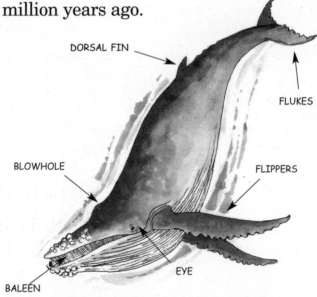

DORSAL FIN

FLUKES

BLOWHOLE

FLIPPERS

BALEEN

EYE

This humpback is a baleen whale.

Whale Classification

Scientists sort plants and animals into different groups or categories. The biggest category is the *kingdom*—the kingdom *Animalia* contains all animals, including humans. After kingdom, the groups get smaller and more specific: *phylum*, *class*, *order*, and *suborder*. Here are the categories that scientists have put whales into:

Kingdom: *Animalia* (all animals)

Phylum: *Chordata* (all animals with back bones)

Class: *Mammalia* (all mammals)

Order: *Cetacea* (all whales)

Suborders: *Mysticeti* (baleen whales) and *Odontoceti* (toothed whales)

The suborders are then split up into even smaller groups, called *families* and *species*.

Orca, or Killer Whale

•Just the Facts•

Scientific Name:	*Orcinus orca*
Suborder:	Toothed whale
Length:	27–33 feet (8–10 m)
Weight:	8,000–12,000 pounds (3,600–5,400 kg)
Where They Live:	Killer whales are found from the tropics to the poles in all oceans.
Food:	Fish, seals, turtles, birds, and even other whales

At 30 feet (9 m) and 10,000 pounds (4,536 kg), the orca is the largest of all dolphins. Orcas are mostly black, but have distinctive white patterns all over their bodies. They have paddlelike flippers and a very big *dorsal* fin. A male orca's dorsal fin can be as tall as 6 feet (1.8 m) They have 40 to 50 large, sharp teeth that are divided between their top and bottom jaws. The teeth are 3 inches (7.6 cm) long.

Orcas live and hunt in a group, known as a *pod.* Some orcas live in one place for most of their lives, and others travel throughout the ocean. The orcas that live in one place are called *resident orcas.* They eat mostly fish. Orcas that travel from one part of the ocean to another are called *transients.* Transient orcas hunt and eat everything, including fish, seals, sea lions, seabirds, and other dolphins and whales. Transient orcas have even been known to attack blue whales. Orcas are very smart hunters and have some tricky ways of catching their prey. In the Arctic, if a seal is on top of an iceberg, orcas can tip over the iceberg by rushing at it and creating a big wave.

When it comes to a baleen whale, big is beautiful!

Chapter 2:
Baleen Whales

Almost all of the really big whales are baleen whales. Most baleen whales range in size from 40 to 100 feet (12–30 m). Even most baleen babies are bigger than you will ever be. Female baleen whales are usually larger than males.

Baleen whales may be the largest animals on Earth, but they feed on some of the smallest. Most baleen whales eat tiny creatures called *zooplankton*. Zooplankton are tiny floating organisms. They drift with water currents, usually in large groups. A few baleen whales also eat small fish.

Some baleen whale adults can eat 8,000 pounds (3,629 kg) of food in one day.

Instead of teeth, baleen whales have large sheets of baleen hanging from their top jaws. Baleen whales scoop up zooplankton in huge quantities, using the baleen in their mouths like a sieve to filter water out and keep prey in. The food gets caught on the baleen fringes, and the water washes back out through the sides of their mouth.

According to my research, baleen works just like a strainer. Water drips out and food stays in.

How Does Baleen Work?

Baleen is a strong but flexible material that grows in sheets or plates from a baleen whale's top jaw. It is made from keratin, the same protein that makes up our fingernails and hair. Each plate has a

Open Wide!

If you thought you could pack a lot into your mouth, think about this: Some bowhead whales' mouths hold up to 700 plates of 14-foot-long (4.5 m) baleen. How do they fit it all in? A bowhead's head can measure over 20 feet (6 m) in length, and its curving mouth goes from its "chin" to near the top of its head.

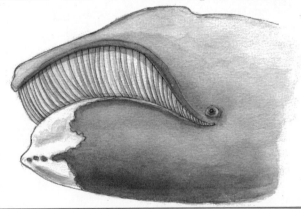

fringed edge and a smooth, straight edge. A baleen whale has several hundred of these plates lined up next to one another, making one long row. All of the fringed edges face toward the tongue. When a whale takes in a huge gulp of water and food, the food gets trapped on the fringed edges of the baleen inside its mouth. The whale pushes the water back out of its mouth and then uses its tongue to lick the food off its baleen.

How Many Baleen Whales Are There?

There are 11 different species, or kinds, of baleen whales in the world. These include right whales such as the southern and northern rights, the pygmy right, and the bowhead; the gray whale; and the rorqual whales.

Blue Whale

·Just the Facts·

Scientific Name:	*Balaenoptera musculus*
Suborder:	Baleen whale
Length:	Average is between 75 and 80 feet (23–24.5 m), but some blue whales have been measured at over 100 feet (30 m). Females are slightly larger than males.
Weight:	Between 110–200 tons (99,800–203,200 kg)
Where They Live:	All oceans
Food:	Krill (tiny shrimplike animals)

Everything about the blue whale is extra-ordinary. It is larger than the biggest dinosaur that ever lived, and it weighs as much as 5,000 seven-year-old human beings or 33 African elephants. Its tongue alone weighs as much as one elephant. Its call is louder than a jet engine. And its heart is the size of a small automobile!

Blue whales do most of their eating in the summer. Most spend the summer months in the colder polar waters, feeding on huge swarms of tiny shrimplike creatures called *krill*. When food is plentiful, a full-grown blue whale eats approximately 40 million krill (that's 4 tons) in one day. In the winter months, blue whales migrate to warmer waters where they mate and raise their young.

Blue whales are often seen alone or in small groups. But some scientists think that they can hear one another from thousands of miles away. So even if a blue whale looks like it's alone, it may be in touch with other blue whales that we can't see.

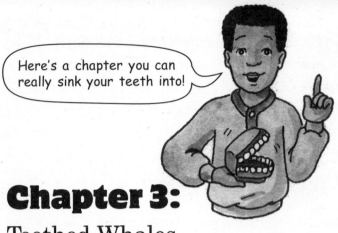

Here's a chapter you can really sink your teeth into!

Chapter 3:
Toothed Whales

One important physical difference between toothed and baleen whales is that toothed whales have teeth instead of baleen. Some toothed whales, like the orca, have many sharp teeth that are good for biting and grasping. Others may only have one or two teeth, or even none at all.

Other differences between toothed and baleen whales are on their heads. On top of their heads, toothed whales only have one blowhole, while baleen whales have two. On their foreheads toothed whales have what looks like a fatty lump. This is actually an important organ called a *melon*. The melon helps to magnify and focus sounds.

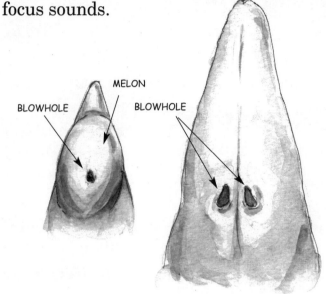

MELON

BLOWHOLE

BLOWHOLE

Toothed whale   Baleen whale

In size, toothed whales range from the 4-foot (1.2 m) harbor porpoise to the 60-foot (18.3 m) sperm whale. Toothed males are generally bigger than toothed females. As you've already read, the opposite is true of baleen whales—female baleen whales are usually larger than the males.

How Do Toothed Whales Behave?

Toothed whales don't just look different from baleen whales, they act differently. Toothed whales tend to be more social than baleen whales. Several types of toothed whales live and hunt together in organized groups called pods. While baleen whales eat huge mouthfuls of small prey, toothed whales hunt and eat larger prey.

> Toothed whales don't chew their food.
> They swallow it whole or in large chunks.

They mostly eat fish, squid, octopus, and cuttlefish.

Toothed whales are active hunters. They have a special ability to "see" and hunt with sound in a process called *echolocation*.

How Many Kinds of Toothed Whales Are There?

There are approximately 68 different kinds of toothed whales. These include dolphins, porpoises, sperm whales, white whales, and beaked whales.

You could say that echolocation is the process of locating objects by using echoes. Here's how it works: A toothed whale can make a variety of sounds, including clicks, whistles, and squeaks. It focuses and directs these sounds to a specific location using the melon, an organ in its forehead. The sounds are usually very high-pitched and travel quickly through water as sound waves. When the sound waves run into an object, like a fish, they bounce off that object and some of them travel back toward the whale as echoes. The echoes travel through the bones in the whale's jaw and reach its inner ear. The toothed whale uses these returning echoes to determine an object's shape, direction, distance, and texture.

What Is a Dolphin?

When you think of dolphins, you probably think of happy animals leaping joyfully through the waves. Did you guess that dolphins are actually a kind of toothed whale? Dolphins are playful and curious, but life at sea is not just fun and games. They have to work hard to find food and watch for enemies.

We Are Family

The dolphin family is the largest and most diverse family of whales. It contains at least 32 different kinds, or species. Dolphins live all over the world, including some species that live in freshwater rivers. Scientists think that dolphins are among the most intelligent and socially complex animals in the world.

What Is a Porpoise?

From the surface, it is difficult to tell dolphins and porpoises apart. But there are differences. Porpoises have flattened and spadelike teeth. Dolphin teeth are shaped like cones and are rounder. While many dolphins have a "beak," porpoises have a blunt snout. Their dorsal (top) fin is shaped like a triangle, while most dolphins have a dorsal fin with a hooklike shape. Finally, porpoises are a little smarter than most dolphins.

Surf's Up!

Why do porpoises and dolphins swim in front of a boat? Are they just having fun? Maybe, but they're also catching a free ride. As a boat moves through the water, it pushes a wave of water ahead of it that's called a *bow wave.* When a porpoise or dolphin rides the bow wave, it is *bow-riding,* and it probably doesn't even have to swim. It just gets pushed along. Scientists believe that some dolphins also bow-ride large whales!

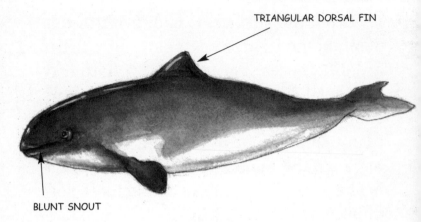

TRIANGULAR DORSAL FIN

BLUNT SNOUT

Porpoise

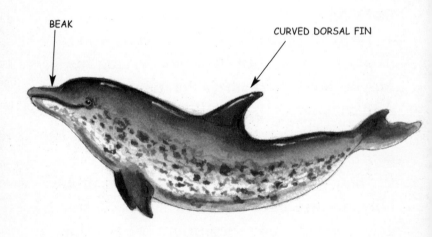

BEAK

CURVED DORSAL FIN

Dolphin

Boto or Amazon River Dolphin

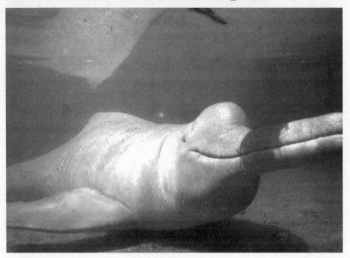

•Just the Facts•

Scientific Name:	*Inia Geoffrensis*
Suborder:	Toothed whale
Length:	7–8.5 feet (2.1–2.6 m)
Weight:	300–350 pounds (136–160 kg)
Where They Live:	Throughout the Amazon and Orinoco River basins
Food:	Fish, river turtles, and crabs

River dolphins are the only whales that live in freshwater. All river dolphins are threatened and some are seriously endangered because they live in places where human activities have affected their habitats and safety.

With its beady eyes, its bulging cheeks, and its long, narrow beak filled with tiny teeth, the Boto is an odd-looking creature. Although their eyesight is better than some other river dolphins, (one in China is almost blind), Botos are thought to rely on echolocation to find their way around. When they do use their eyes, they will swim upside down to see the bottom of the river better. Boto dolphins can be blue-gray, off-white, or even pink!

That whale has a whale of an appetite!

Chapter 4:

The Search for Food

One thing whales have in common is that they like to eat—a *lot*. But each kind of whale has a special diet and a unique method of catching its food, and a mouth built to deal with its meals.

How Do Baleen Whales Find Food?

Baleen whales move through the ocean looking for large masses of food. In the summer, many baleen whales in the northern hemisphere swim toward the Arctic, where they *graze,* or feed, on pastures of *plankton*. Plankton are tiny organisms that drift at or near the surface of the ocean.

Plankton pastures can be hundreds of miles wide and thousands of miles long. That's enough food for even the biggest whales.

There is so much food that most baleen whales eat enough during the summer months that they can live mostly off their fat reserves for the rest of the year. That way, they don't have to track down food in the winter.

How do baleen whales know where to find their food in the huge ocean? Scientists aren't exactly sure. If a food supply is in the same place year after year, whales probably remember where this food is. But they also use their senses. They may see, taste, smell, or even hear food.

Wouldn't it be strange if you could find pizza or a peanut butter and jelly sandwich by listening for them? Well, that may be exactly how baleen whales find their favorite foods. There is, however, one big difference between the food you eat and the food baleen whales eat—their food is alive and moving. Even though an individual krill (the food of blue whales) is tiny, when krill are in a mass of millions, blue whales can probably hear their movements from several miles away.

How Do Baleen Whales Catch Their Food?

Each kind of baleen whale catches its food in a unique way.

Rorquals, like the blue whale, are *gulpers*. A rorqual gulps in tremendous amounts of water and food, expanding its mouth and throat like a balloon. Then it squeezes out the water and uses its tongue to scrape off the food that's left behind. Humpbacks, another kind of rorqual, are gulpers, too. They some-

A blue whale can hold 1,000 tons or more of water and food in its mouth and throat. This allows it to catch up to 4 tons of food in one day. That's 8,000 pounds (3,630 kg), or 36,000 quarter-pound hamburgers.

times blow "nets," or clouds of bubbles, below or around a school of fish. The bubbles confuse the fish and make them swim in a smaller and smaller circle. The humpbacks will then lunge up through their "bubble nets," catching more fish than they might have otherwise. Some humpback whales also use their tails to slap the water before they begin feeding. Scientists think this scares and stuns the fish, making them easier to catch.

Bowhead and other right whales are *skimmers*. They cruise along the surface of the water with their mouths open, catching whatever is unlucky enough to be in the way.

Gray whales are *slurpers*. They swim in shallow ocean waters and dive to the bottom to dine, where they stir up mud and sand to get at their favorite foods.

How Do Toothed Whales Find Their Food?

Toothed whales are hunters. They actively search for prey and then catch it. You've already learned that toothed whales often use sound or echolocation to learn about what's around them. They also use echolocation to find food.

Whales aren't the only animals that can echolocate. Bats, golden hamsters, shrews, and flying lemurs all search for food using the same method.

Some scientists think that certain toothed whales can use echolocation as a weapon to stun fish or other prey. They have heard dolphins make hundreds or even thousands of high clicks per second when they spot a school of fish. As the clicks reach them, the fish seem stunned and confused, which gives the dolphins time to sweep in and scoop up a tasty meal.

Master Blasters

Some dolphins can send as many as 2,000 echolocation clicks per second. From the returning echoes, a dolphin can detect a fish from far away. In fact, scientists have found that dolphins can use their echolocation on objects 2 inches (5 cm) or smaller, up to 650 feet (200 m) away!

How Else Do Toothed Whales Hunt?

Toothed whales don't always use

echolocation to find food. If food is close by and near the surface of the ocean, whales can see their next meal with their eyes.

Silence Is Golden

If a toothed whale wants to sneak up on its prey, making noises that the prey could hear might not always be the best solution. Orcas, or killer whales, usually stay silent as they sneak up on seals or other prey, and probably use mostly their eyesight, instead of echolocation.

Some toothed whales hunt in places where their eyes are of little or no use. Sperm whales hunt at depths of over 3,000 feet below the surface. At this depth, there is almost no light. So sperm whales rely completely on echolocation to sense squid, their primary prey.

Do Toothed Whales Ever Cooperate to Hunt?

Some kinds of dolphins work as a group to catch prey. Several dozen dolphins may form a circle around a school of fish, making it nearly impossible for the fish to escape. Once they have trapped the fish, the dolphins will take turns lunging into the ball of panicked fish to feed.

Go Fish!

In the town of Laguna, Brazil, fishermen and bottlenose dolphins work together to catch fish. The fishermen line up in the shallow ocean waters along the shore, waiting with fishing nets. One or two dolphins swim near the men, facing the sea and looking for signs of fish. When they see fish, they dive into the water and drive the fish toward the fishermen's nets. The dolphins get a tasty reward for their help: They feed on any of the fish that the fishermen don't catch.

Bottlenose dolphins are famous for working as a team to herd fish.

Do Toothed Whales Chew Their Food?

Most toothed whales don't chew their food, at least not the way you do. In fact, most toothed whales

Some toothed whales don't use teeth to eat. They use suction, like a vacuum cleaner, to capture squid, fish, and other smaller prey.

swallow their food whole. When their prey is too large for this, they will rip it apart into pieces that are small enough to swallow. The whales can eat many more fish by not taking the time to chew!

An orca can eat 551 pounds (250 kg) of food in one day. Now that's an appetite!

Gray Whale

•Just the Facts•

Scientific Name: *Eschrichtius robustus*

Suborder: Baleen whale

Length: Average is between 35–50 feet (11–15 m). Adult females are usually a little larger than males.

Weight: Both sexes weigh 20–40 tons (27,200–36,300 kg)

Where It Lives: Only in the North Pacific. Gray whales used to live in the North Atlantic, but were driven to extinction there by whaling.

Food: Mostly small crustaceans called *amphipods*

The gray whale is a one-of-a-kind animal and is unique enough to be classified in a separate family from all other whales. Some scientists believe it to be the most primitive of living whales and to have been around for more than 100,000 years. Some gray whales carry as many as a half ton of *barnacles* on their bodies. Barnacles are tiny parasitic animals that attach themselves to objects such as rocks, ships, or whales.

Each year, gray whales travel between 8,000 and 12,000 miles (12,875–19,312 km) back and forth between their feeding groups in the Arctic to breeding grounds off the coast of Baja California. During its lifetime, the average gray whale commutes over 400,000 miles (643,700 km)—the equivalent of a trip to the moon and back.

The gray whale doesn't need to eat on these long trips. It can go without food for so long because it stores energy in its layers of blubber.

How would you act if *you* were a whale?

Chapter 5:
Whale Behaviors

When your mother tells you to behave, what is she really saying? Is she telling you to mind your manners or to act like a human being? Maybe both. But when scientists talk about how whales behave, they are talking about how whales act and react to their environment, other animals, and one another. A whale's behavior has a lot to do with its senses. Whales use sight, sound, touch, taste, and, in some cases, smell to learn about the world around them and decide what to do. They also use their senses to communicate. Whales don't have language the same way humans do, but they send one another messages in other ways.

Sight

Most whales can see well—in some cases, their eyesight is as good as yours. But sometimes water is murky or, if they dive more than 300 feet (91 m) below the surface, there is not enough light to see by. When that happens, whales need to use other senses.

To See or Not to See?

It depends what whale you're talking about. A blue whale's eyes are each the size of a large grapefruit. But the Ganges River dolphin's two eyes are only the size of a small pea. This dolphin lives in a murky river where sight is almost useless, so it primarily uses echolocation to navigate and hunt.

Touch

Whales have a good sense of touch. Whales, dolphins, and porpoises touch one another to send messages.

If a dolphin rakes its teeth against another dolphin, it can be a sign of displeasure or a way of bossing the second dolphin around. It may also be a way for two dolphins to signal to each other that they would like to mate.

When a baby dolphin pushes its melon up against the mother's mammary glands (the glands that produce milk), it's a signal to the mother that the baby is ready to feed.

Have you ever noticed how a cat's whiskers quiver when they touch something? A cat uses its whiskers to sense objects or movements. Some baleen whales do have hairy bristles near their mouths and at the front of their heads. Scientists think whales use these bristles the same way a cat uses its whiskers.

Hearing

All whales have excellent hearing, and ears and brains that are well adapted for hearing underwater.

You've already learned that toothed whales can echolocate, or produce sound and use its echo to "see" their environment and other animals. Baleen whales also may use sound and its echoes in other ways. A blue whale's calls, for instance, may bounce off landmasses and echo back to the blue whale. The whale then may use this information to navigate.

Many scientists think that whales may have a built-in compass that they use to help them navigate the oceans. This "compass" helps them sense the earth's magnetic fields and know which direction is north and south.

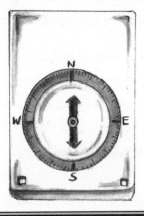

Whales use many different sounds to communicate. Some whales grunt, groan, and make noises like a creaking door. Others can sing, chirp, and whistle. What do all these noises mean? It depends on the whale and the situation.

Sperm whales produce clicks in patterns called *codas* that are almost like Morse code. Different codas have different meanings. One might be a way of saying hello. Another might be a request for help or a way of saying, "Knock it off."

Some scientists think that dolphins use whistles, clicks, squeals, and noises that sound almost like barking to communicate. Each dolphin has its own special whistle, called a *signature whistle*. A dolphin's signature whistle is almost like a name, but instead of saying, "Hi, my name is Brett," the dolphin whistles.

Scientists who study orcas have learned that pods, or groups of orcas, each have their own distinctive dialect, or variation, of sounds. The more closely

If you examine a whale, you will not see anything that resembles an ear—at least not on the outside of its head. Whales' ears are inside their heads.

Mother bottlenose dolphins whistle to their babies very often. Scientists think this is so the baby will get to know the sound of its mother's voice.

related orcas are to one another, the more similar their sounds will be.

Some baleen whales sing. The most famous singer is the humpback whale. Only male humpback whales sing, and they only sing during the winter months to attract mates. Their songs are made up of several simple themes or melodies that they sing over and over again.

Play It Again

A humpback's song can last from a few minutes to a half hour. When a humpback reaches the end, it starts all over again. One humpback was recorded singing continuously for more than 22 hours!

Taste

Whales have taste buds, although their sense of taste is not as strong as humans'. They have been known to spit out food that, apparently, doesn't taste right to them.

A whale can also taste seawater to sense the presence of other whales.

Body Language

Whales, dolphins, and porpoises have many nonverbal ways to send a message. When they're excited, angry, or upset, dolphins sometimes blow bubbles. When a whale is angry or upset, it may slap its tail on the water.

• **Breaching:**

Some whales, such as the humpback, jump high into the air and then crash back into the water with a huge splash. This is called *breaching*. Some scientists think it's a way of showing off. Others think whales breach to get barnacles,

There are many theories as to why whales breach, but no one really knows.

lice, and other irritating parasites off their bodies. Sometimes, it may just be a whale's way of saying, "Isn't life a blast!"

- **Lobtailing:**

Whales slap their tails on the water for different reasons. This is called lobtailing. Sometimes, a whale will slap its tail to tell other whales, "This is my territory, stay away." Or, if a mother is upset with her *calf* (baby), she will sometimes slap her tail on the water. Whales also use tail slapping to stun fish right before they catch them.

> Some southern right whales use their large tails to sail in the wind. Scientists think they do this just for the fun of it.

- **Spy hopping:**

When a whale lifts its head vertically up out of the water so that its eyes are just above the water line, this is called *spy hopping*. This is probably not a way of communicating with other whales, but it is a way to take a good look around.

Beluga Whale

•Just the Facts•

Scientific Name: *Delphinapterus leucas*

Suborder: Toothed whale

Length: 10–15 feet (3–4.6 m)

Weight: 3,000–3,300 pounds (1,360–1,500 kg)

Where They Live: Only in the Arctic and sub-Arctic

Food: Fish, squid, octopi, worms, crab, or shrimp

Belugas live in large herds, called pods, in the cold polar waters. In summer, they go north to feed in the rich Arctic waters. In winter, they swim farther south to avoid being trapped in ice. Belugas often follow bowhead whales, since bowheads use their thick skulls to break a path through sheets of ice. Belugas are sometimes found in groups of more than 1,000 whales. One reason they may move in such large groups is as a form of protection against their two main predators—polar bears and orcas.

Beluga means "white one" in Russian. Its scientific name means "white whale without fins." Sailors used to call belugas "the canaries of the sea" because they make so much noise. Belugas can squeal, whistle, groan, and produce a wide range of clicks.

Unlike most whales, belugas have flexible necks and can turn their heads. Their faces are much more expressive than most whales'. When a beluga purses its lips, it looks like it's saying, "Oh."

Whales have families, just like you. (Well, maybe not *just* like you...)

Chapter 6:
Whale Families

Just as there are different kinds of human families, there are different kinds of whale families. For many kinds of whales, a "family" is a mother and her baby. Blue whales, for instance, are rarely seen in groups except when a mother is with her baby, or calf. But sperm whales live in groups of many females and their calves.

Between the ages of 6 and 10, male sperm whales leave the group and go off to join other young males in their own group. Later in life, male sperm whales go off on their own. They only return to a group when they

Orcas stay with their mothers for their entire life, only leaving briefly to mate.

are ready to have babies of their own.

In general, toothed whales are much more social than baleen whales and live together in larger groups.

Let's Get Together

Dolphins who live way out in the ocean, far away from land, sometimes form groups of more than 10,000. They socialize and play together, but also cooperate in hunting and fighting off predators.

Whale Babies

When a baby whale is born, it swims right to the surface of the ocean to get its first gasp of air. Baby whales are born knowing how to swim, but they are not nearly as graceful or as strong as their mothers. Often, a calf will swim by its mother's side. Some kinds of whales even hitch a ride on their mother's back for the first few days.

Some whale calves swim next to their mothers. That way, the mother's movement pulls the calf along.

A Built-in Baby Carrier

A mother finless porpoise has a patch of rough skin on her back covered with wartlike bumps. These make it easy for the baby to fit snugly, even when the mom dives or rises up to the surface.

Baby whales stay very close to their mothers for the first several months of their life. Males are rarely, if ever, involved in raising their children. Sometimes a mother gets help from other female whales. After a beluga calf is born, a "baby-sit-

> Female Baird's beaked whales carry their young for up to 17 months before giving birth. That's almost twice as long as humans!

ter" might help the mother protect the calf for the first few weeks. And when a mother sperm whale dives for food, other female whales watch her calf while she's gone.

Baby whales are a lot like human babies in some ways. For one thing, they're always hungry. A baby blue whale can drink up to 100 gallons (378 L) of its mother's milk and can gain over 200 pounds (91 kg) in one day! The whale mom squirts milk straight into its baby's mouth. Gray whales sometimes even hold their babies between their flippers while they nurse.

Whale milk is about 20 to 40 percent fat and full of nutrients. It is said to taste like a mixture of fish, liver, milk of magnesia, and caster oil. Blech!

Whale calves love to play. A gray whale often uses its mother as a huge playground, sliding off her back, rolling across her tail, or simply rubbing up against her. Other baby whales will surf the waves, toss around objects they find in the ocean (or sometimes even small animals!), or spin around in circles.

A Living Playpen

Bottlenose dolphins that are traveling through the open ocean will often form "playpens" for their calves by positioning themselves around the calves in a "U" or "L" shape. This helps protect the calves from any predators that may be around.

How Long Do Calves Stay with Their Mothers?

Life in the ocean is difficult for a young whale. There are a lot of dangers and even more things to learn. A whale mother tries to protect and feed her calf for as long as possible. But when a mother is ready to have another baby, she needs to stop nursing her first one.

Whales have babies every two to six years.

Baby whales stay with their mothers for anywhere from half a year to their entire life. A fin whale goes off by itself after seven or eight months. But an orca stays with its mother and her pod for its entire life. A dolphin calf will stick by its mom's side for about one year. It probably stops nursing after a few years, but remains by its mother's side. The calf learns how to hunt, avoid predators, and get along with other dolphins. After that, a dolphin calf will adopt a new "family," or pod.

Certain kinds of whales seem to find a best friend and stick with him or her. Bottlenose male dolphins tend to stick together, and scientists have seen several pairs of gray whales together over several years. Saddle and Whitepatch are two gray whales that people have spotted together for several years in a row off the coast of Vancouver Island.

Sperm Whales

•Just the Facts•

Scientific Name: *Physeter macrocephalus*

Suborder: Toothed whale

Length: Males: 50–60 feet long (15–18 m);
Females: 33–40 feet (10–12 m)

Weight: Males: 40–50 tons
(36,287–45,359 kg); Females:
14–18 tons (12,701–16,329 kg)

Where They Live: In all oceans, but they are rarely
found in coastal waters

Food: Mainly squid, but also octopi and
some kinds of fish

The sperm whale is the largest toothed whale and the deepest diver of any marine mammal. It routinely dives to depths of 3,000 to 4,000 feet (914–1,219 m) to catch deepwater squid and has been recorded diving to depths as great as 9,200 feet (2,804 m), or almost 2 miles.

The sperm whale is an imposing and strange-looking creature. Its huge, box-shaped head is between one-quarter and one-third of the whale's body length. Its head houses the biggest brain in the world. A sperm whale's brain weighs about 20 pounds and is as large as a basketball!

The sperm whale got its name from the huge amount of spermaceti oil in its head. Its scientific name, *Physeter macrocephalus,* means "long-headed blower."

Sperm whales are the most social of the large whales. Females and young whales live in groups of 10 to 20 in warm waters throughout the year. Males leave the group between ages 6 and 10 and move to cooler waters. The juvenile males form a group known as a "bachelor school." Once they reach about age 27, males go off on their own and only rejoin a group during mating season.

It's time to make the world safe for whales!

Chapter 7:

Whaling and Other Dangers

The ocean, home to almost all of the world's whales, dolphins, and porpoises, covers 72 percent of Earth's surface. It is a beautiful and mysterious place. For whales, it can also be a dangerous one. Whales have few natural predators, except for killer whales and, in rare cases, sharks. But they do have an unlikely enemy—humans. Human activities pose a serious threat to whales everywhere.

Whaling, or hunting whales, has made some whale species endangered.

Man-made pollution can kill whales or make them very sick. Fishing with huge nets that catch dolphins as well as fish has depleted some dolphin populations by more than 50 percent. Boat traffic and the noise that our boats make can also cause problems for these animals. Even people who care about whales and dolphins can hurt them accidentally. When people take their boats too close to the dolphins and whales, or try to swim with them and touch them, it puts the animals in danger.

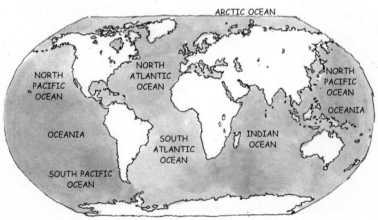

Whales live in oceans all over the world, but in many places they are in danger.

There are several species of cetaceans whose numbers are less than 300 and are shrinking. The Baiji river dolphin lives in the Yangtze River in China and is severely endangered. Only about 50 to 250 Baiji dolphins remain today. The Baiji is threatened by fishing, dams, pollution, and run-ins with boat propellers.

The Vaquita or Gulf of California harbor porpoise numbers around 200 remaining animals. This small porpoise gets tangled in illegally set fishing nets.

But there is some good news. Many scientists, government officials, and ordinary people are working hard to make the ocean a safer place for whales. Many laws now make certain kinds of ocean pollution illegal. *Sanctuaries,* or protected areas, are being created in places where dolphins and whales breed. And most countries in the world have stopped whaling. Currently, only Japan and Norway continue to hunt whales. Native peoples such as the Makah and the Inuit also hunt whales in limited numbers according to old traditions and customs.

Whaling

People have hunted whales for many centuries. At first, people threw wooden harpoons (long, sharp, spearlike weapons) at whales from the shore or from small

boats. This was very dangerous for humans, as a whale could destroy a small boat with a flick of its tail. But it was worth the risk to a village or community, since one whale could provide enough food and other important products to last an entire winter. These early people needed to hunt whales in order to survive. But over the years, many people discovered that hunting whales could also make them a lot of money.

Whaling for money, or commercial whaling, began in the twelfth century. The Basques, people who live in northern

Spain, hunted right whales in the Bay of Biscay. The Basques were great seamen and explorers, and by the sixteenth century they had expanded their whaling activities to distant oceans.

In the seventeenth century, Holland became the next great whaling power. Then, in the eighteenth century, the English and New Englanders stepped in. Whaling was still very dangerous, and many whalers died at sea. But whaling was a quick way to get rich if you got lucky.

By this time, whale products had become very valuable. Baleen was used to make household objects like hairbrushes, umbrellas, brooms, and corsets. Oil was used to lubricate machines and to light streetlamps.

In the nineteenth century, two inventions made whaling much easier for people—and much harder for whales.

Norwegian whalers created a powerful harpoon gun that made it easier to kill whales. And, by the end of that century, the small boats that went into the water to catch whales were able to use engines. They could follow a whale until it became exhausted.

Whaler's Gold

The most valuable part of a whale was *ambergris*, a hard, waxy substance sometimes produced in the large intestine of a sperm whale. Sperm whales are the only animals that produce this substance. Ambergris was, at one time, considered more valuable than gold. Why would a glob of sort of smelly stuff from a whale's intestines be valuable? It was used for fixing scents in expensive perfumes. There was nothing else in the world that worked as well. These days, chemists have found other substances that do the trick.

During the first half of the twentieth century, things only got worse for the whales. Their oil was still very valuable. It was no longer used for lighting (electricity had replaced whale oil) but to make soap, margarine, and many other products. New inventions helped whalers catch faster whales that they hadn't been able to kill before. In 1931, 30,000 blue whales were killed just in the Antarctic Ocean.

In the second half of the twentieth century, people realized that the whale population was shrinking, and that we would have to try to protect whales if we didn't want them to become endangered or extinct. Over the years, many nations have agreed to limit their whaling activities or to stop altogether. Scientists and environmental groups try to educate the public about the dangers that whales face.

They're Not Saved Yet

People have worked hard to save the whales, but that does not mean they're out of danger. At least 10 species of dolphins, porpoises, and whales are still endangered. All whales face the threats of chemical and noise pollution and destruction of their homes.

How can you help? Just learning about whales and sharing your knowledge will raise awareness. There are also national and international organizations that are devoted to saving and helping whales. Here are two that you can contact to find out how you can help:

Pacific Whale Foundation
101 N. Kihei Road
Kihei, HI 96753
http://www.pacificwhale.org/about/in-
dex.html

The American Cetacean Society
P.O. Box 1391
San Pedro, CA 90733-1391
http://www.acsonline.org/

If you live near the ocean or will be visiting an ocean soon, you can also find out about whale-watching trips. There are books and websites about whale watching that list whale-watching expeditions.

Northern and Southern Right Whales

Scientific Names: *Eubalaena glacialis* and *Eubalaena australis*

Suborder: Baleen whale

Length: Average is between 49–56 feet (15–17 m).

Weight: Approximately 50–60 tons (36,300–54,000 kg)

Where They Live: Northern right whales live in the western North Atlantic and the western North Pacific. Southern right whales live in the southern hemisphere, including the South Atlantic, South Pacific, Antarctic, and southern Indian Ocean.

Food: Mostly small crustaceans (ocean creatures with shells) called *copepods*

Right whales were given their unfortunate name by whalers who considered them the "right" whales to catch. They were very valuable: a nineteenth-century hunter could make a lot of money from selling a right whale's oil and long, silky baleen. They were slow moving, swam close to shore, and were easy to spot, which made right whales easier to catch than most other whales.

Because they were overhunted for many centuries, right whales are now considered endangered. There are only approximately 300 northern right whales left today. Southern right whales have fared slightly better and number between 3,000 and 4,000.

Where humans might have hair, right whales have patches of rough skin called *callosities*. Millions of whale lice find their home on callosities. The callosities on top of a right whale's head are known as bonnets. Each right whale has a different-looking bonnet. Whale researchers can identify individual whales by their *bonnets*.

Think you know everything there is to know about whales? Think again.

Chapter 8:
Whale of a Fact

Whales are amazing creatures. What's even more amazing is how much we still have to learn about them. Here are some whale facts and feats that are sure to wow you.

Record Breakers:

- Bowheads have the longest baleen of all baleen whales. They have a highly arched mouth suited to the huge baleen, which may grow as long as 13 to 15 feet (4 m). If laid end to end, the

Bowheads have a layer of blubber that is 1½ to 2 feet (45.7–61 cm) thick. This keeps them warm and toasty in those cold Arctic seas.

plates of one bowhead would stretch over 1 mile (1.6 km).

- Bowheads not only have long baleen, but unusually hard heads. Their skulls are so thick they can use their heads to break through ice one foot (30 cm) thick. Why would bowheads bother butting ice? These large whales live year-round in the Arctic and often need to break through ice so they can breathe.

- Don't flip out, but humpback whales have the longest flippers of any whale. Humpback flippers are one-third the size of their bodies, or as long as 17 feet (5 m)! Their flippers are so long, some people think they look like giant wings.

- Spinner dolphins seem to love leaping into the air and spinning around. Spinners can spin more than a dozen times in a row before splashing back down into the ocean.
- You already know that sperm whales can dive almost 2 miles (3.2 km) deep, but did you know they can stay

underwater for more than an hour at a time?

- Scientists have recently found a new way to estimate the age of bowhead whales. They have found at least one whale that was over 200 years old when it died. Most large whales live to be 50 to 80 years old.

Body of Knowledge

- You already know that a blue whale is huge. Its mouth can hold 50 bathtubs full of water at once. But did you know that a blue whale's throat is no larger than your own? No wonder its favorite food is krill no bigger than your pinkie!
- The skin of a blue whale has been measured at about 225 square yards (188 sq m). This would cover an entire tennis court.
- It has been calculated that a single breath from a mature blue whale could inflate 2,000 balloons.

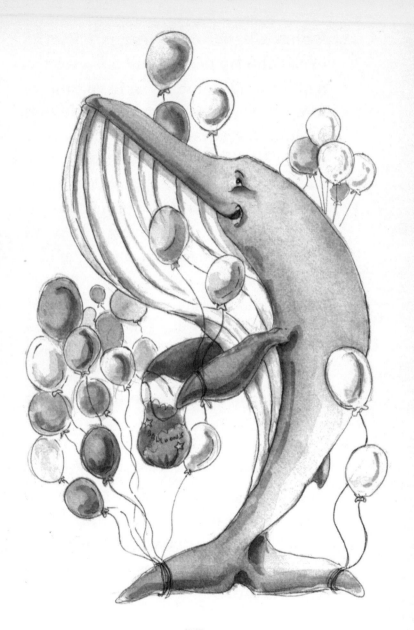

- A blue whale's outer ear is only the size of the tip of a pencil!
- Whales' and dolphins' skin is always being shed and replaced. A bottlenose dolphin, for example, replaces its outermost layer of skin every two hours.
- Want to figure out the age of a whale? If it's a baleen whale, you can count the plugs of wax in its ear. If it's a toothed whale, you can count the layers in its teeth!
- Whales don't have vocal cords. So how do they make clicks, squeals, and whistles? A whale has pouches of air near its blowhole. Special muscles squeeze these pouches to set up vibrations that produce sounds.
- Male narwhal whales have one tooth that grows straight out of their mouths and can be up to 10 feet (3 m) long. It grows in spirals and looks like a tusk. The narwhal's tusk may be the basis for the legend of the unicorn. Hundreds of years ago, when

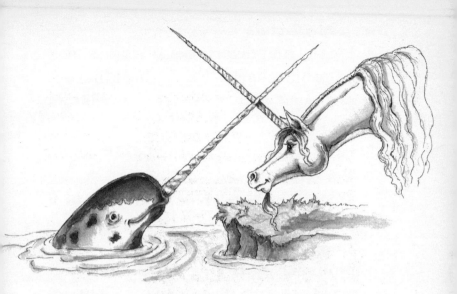

European traders came back from the far parts of the world with narwhal teeth, they either didn't know or didn't want to give away the real source of the long, twisting tusks. People may have dreamed up the unicorn to explain these "horns."

- Humpback whales have distinctive black and white markings on their tails, or flukes. Each humpback's markings are so distinctive, they're like fingerprints.

- Pygmy and dwarf sperm whales look a bit like sharks. Their sharklike appearance may help scare predators away.
- Gray whales, which migrate along the west coast of North America, are able to swim in water as shallow as 6 feet (1.8 m).
- Franciscana or La Plate River dolphins have the longest beak (in relation to their body size) of any dolphin.
- Because of their pale-colored bodies and their shy nature toward humans, Franciscana dolphins are known to fishermen as "the white ghost."
- Indus and Ganges river dolphins have the strange habit of swimming on one side, trailing one flipper in the mud to search for food. They can also be seen swimming with just their beaks sticking straight out of the water.
- Indus river dolphins are called *susu* by people who live near the Indus

River, in Pakistan. Susu is meant to sound like the sneezelike breathing sound these dolphins make.

- Finless porpoises don't have a dorsal (back) fin, but they do have two pectoral fins, or flippers.

About half the finless porpoises in the world have pink eyes!

- The Irrawaddy dolphin is considered a sacred animal by fishermen in Vietnam. If they catch a dolphin in their nets, they will free it, and, in areas along the Mekong River, they will cremate a dead dolphin and give it a religious ceremony in respect! In at least one river village the dolphins help fishermen by rounding up fish and driving them into the nets.

The Weird and the Wonderful

- Whales don't sweat.
- Because a whale's weight is supported by water, its skeleton is lighter than those of land animals that are the same size. If an elephant's skeleton, for instance, were as light as that of a whale of similar size, it wouldn't be able to stand up, but would collapse.

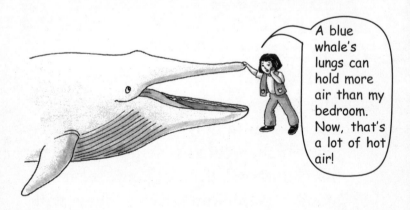

A blue whale's lungs can hold more air than my bedroom. Now, that's a lot of hot air!

- An echolocating whale or dolphin can detect not just the shape of an object, but what's inside it. So if you were diving near a whale or dolphin, it might "see" your skeleton and what you ate for lunch that day!
- Sperm whales have been found with giant squid, measuring over 35 feet (11 m), in their stomachs.
- Some whales can pick up underwater sounds from 1,000 miles (1,600 km) away or farther.

Strap-toothed whale

•Just the Facts•

Scientific Name: *Mesoplodon layardii*

Suborder: Toothed whale

Length: 16–20 feet (5–6 m)

Weight: 1–3 tons (907–2,721 kg)

Where They Live: The southern hemisphere. They have been found most frequently in New Zealand and Australia, but have also been recorded in South Africa, Namibia, the Falkland Islands, Argentina, Chile, and Uruguay.

Food: Squid and possibly octopi

Scientists know less about beaked whales than any other group of whales in the world. These whales live far out in the ocean, dive to great depths, and don't often come into contact with humans. In fact, we only know about some kinds of beaked whales because people have discovered them after they've died and washed up on shore. Not very many people have ever seen a living strap-toothed whale. The strangest thing about the strap-toothed whale is that the male has two teeth growing up out of its mouth. As a male strap-toothed whale gets older, its teeth curl over its top jaw. The teeth of a male strap-toothed whale can be as long as 12 inches (30 cm).

A male's teeth can get so long and curved that it becomes impossible for the whale to open its mouth very far! Fortunately, a strap-toothed whale can still catch squid by sucking them into its mouth.

INDEX